Poems from Both Sides of the Fence

Poems from Both Sides of the Fence

Beryl B. Lawn, M.D.

Texas Review Press
Huntsville, Texas

FIRST EDITION, 2011
Requests for permission to reproduce material from this
work should be sent to:

Permissions
Texas Review Press
English Department
Sam Houston State University
Huntsville, TX 77341-2146

Acknowledgements:

Front-cover photo by Ronnie Thweatt, The Studio—Temple, Texas
Front-cover graphic by Kwik Kopy—Temple, Texas
Cover design by Nancy Parsons, Graphic Design Group

Library of Congress Cataloging-in-Publication Data

Lawn, Beryl B.
  Poems from both sides of the fence : a disabled
physician's experiences in medicine / Beryl B. Lawn. -- 1st
ed.
        p. cm.
  Originally published by B.B.L. Publications in 2009?
  ISBN 978-1-933896-56-4 (pbk. : alk. paper)
  1. Lawn, Beryl B. 2. Women physicians--United States--
Poetry. 3. Women physicians--United States--Biography.
4. Women with disabilities--United States--Poetry. 5.
Women with disabilities--United States--Biography. 6.
Physicians--United States--Biography. 7. People with
disabilities--United States--Biography. I. Title.
  R692.L39 2011
  610.82--dc22
                                    2011008156

In memory of
W. Geoffrey Lawn

CONTENTS

Poems from Both Sides of the Fence

CULTURAL INCOMPETENCE

When I was nine,
my family moved
from Texas
to Israel.
On my first day
of 4th grade
in my new school,
the boy next to me
in assembly
nudged me
and whispered
"Do you believe
in Jesus?"
"Sure," I answered
(who didn't?)
The repercussions
of that answer
were my first (painful)
lessons in
cultural diversity.

VISIONS

When I was fourteen,
I started seeing
spider webs.
"Her vision's normal,"
the optician
told my mother.
I said no more,
but continued
watching the webs
as they tossed and turned
when I moved my eyes.
In college,
I feared I was
schizophrenic, "seeing things."
"Floaters,"
the ophthalmologist called them,
"nothing to worry about."
I sobbed.
I wasn't going blind.
And I wasn't
schizophrenic.

FORK IN THE ROAD

The burglar kicks
the door in,
and I, escaping,
fall from
the 3rd floor fire ladder
and,
broken,
lie below.
He meanwhile
takes only my
best jewelry,
leaving the rest
behind.

THE INTERVIEW

I was injured
and now walk
with braces and crutches.
When I schedule
the job interview,
I don't mention
the braces and crutches.
The receptionist
asks me to
have a seat
for a moment,
then returns
to tell me that
the position
has already
been filled.

FRONT ROW SEAT

On the first day
of my first week
in medical school,
one of our
orientation speakers
observed
that as physicians
we would be
given a special
honor:
A front row seat
in the theater
of life.
Never
in my wildest imagination
could I have
forecast
the accuracy of
his prediction.

STORIES

Studs Terkel,
an oral history expert,
says everyone has
a story—
even (especially!)
the janitor
or the clerk
at Walmart.
We are surrounded
by stories,
whole novels, even—
all we
have to do
is listen!

REGRET

When I was a medical student,
an 8-year-old girl
was brought to pediatrics
with a vaginal discharge.
It was 1970.
Childhood sexual abuse
wasn't even
on the radar.
I can't remember
what we told
her mom —
something nonspecific
and reassuring,
as I recall.
In later years I've wondered
what that child's
real story was,
and how badly
(as I fear)
we failed her.

WHEELCHAIR

Some people
describe me
as being
confined
to a wheelchair.
I believe
I am
set free
by my wheelchair.

SURPRISE

A 12-year-old girl
came to the E.R.
complaining of
severe stomach cramps.
"She hasn't
been to school
in three days,"
her distraught mother
added.
We examined the girl:
she was
eight months
pregnant.

HUBRIS

"It's because you
don't want to be
a woman,"
the student-health doctor
told my patient
when she went
to see him
for menstrual cramps.
He did not
examine her.
Five years later
she discovers
she has
advanced endometriosis
and needs
a hysterectomy.

GUILT

I am an intern
and discover that
my patient,
admitted for
something else,
has a weak right arm.
"Arthritis in his neck
compressing the nerves,"
the neurosurgeons
say. "We can
fix it."
I am grateful.
During surgery,
a complication:
the patient is
left paralyzed.
I do not go
to see him.

BAD NEWS

Doctors don't like
giving bad news.
They're not trained
to do it.
The patient
may be devastated.
(Besides, who likes
talking about
death?)
The patient may blame
the doctor.
(The doctor already
feels he has failed
anyway).
The patient may
"lose it."
The doctor may
"lose it."
Best to ignore
the whole thing:
start another course
of treatment.
Doctors don't like
giving bad news.

RACIST RECTAL EXAM

It was the height
of the civil rights era,
and a patient
wrote a letter
to my chairman
accusing me
of performing
a "racist rectal exam."
I was unaware
of having done
anything unusual.
Although the chairman
did not ask me to,
I met with the patient
and told her
I was sorry.

DREAM DIAGNOSIS

I had a patient
with puzzling symptoms:
poorly controlled hypertension,
renal failure,
stiff joints.
I had a dream
one night
in which it was revealed that
the patient had scleroderma.
This diagnosis
ultimately proved correct.
It also proved to be
my only—
ever—
dream diagnosis.

CHOICE

Nietzsche says
the possibility of suicide
gets us through
many a dark night.
What got me through
my internship
was the possibility
of walking away.
"If one more bad thing
happens, I'll
simply walk away
and never come back,"
I tell myself
on yet another
36-hour day.
It was a mental game
giving the illusion of control,
an emergency exit
which just by
being there
precluded my need
to use it.

CONSCIENTIOUSNESS

The patient was being evaluated
for fever of unknown origin.
All the doctors
were stymied.
The med student
said he heard
an aortic insufficiency murmur.
The staff rolled their eyes
and chuckled . . . .
. . . but listened . . . .
and they too
heard an aortic insufficiency murmur.
The patient had endocarditis.
The student made the diagnosis.
How?
By simply spending ten minutes
listening to
the heart.

LUNCH

A hotdog vendor
had his cart
on the corner
below our 2nd floor
medical office.
He usually
blew his nose
sans handkerchief.
"Hold the mustard,"
my partner yells.

GENDER-IDENTITY ISSUES

A young man
came to the E.R.
carrying his severed
penis
in his hand,
having reconsidered
his actions.
A previous classmate
of mine,
a urologist,
re-attached it
with
passable results
I am told.

SKIN

When I was an intern,
a young college student
died of psoriasis.
We forget our skin:
it doesn't have
the cachet
of the heart,
or kidneys,
yet is every
bit as necessary.
It holds in moisture,
screens out germs,
shivers to warm us,
and cools us with sweat.
A workhorse of the body,
appreciated only for
her beauty.

ASSUMPTIONS

Looking at me
sitting in my
wheelchair,
you see someone
ineffectual,
unemployed,
unhappy,
poor,
alone.
The man alongside me
must be
my attendant.
You don't see
my well-paying job,
home in the 'burbs,
happy marriage.
All there is to know
about me
is not inscribed
on the wheels
of my
chair.

DELAY IN TREATMENT

As an intern
in an inner-city E.R.,
I was used to
seeing
disease in its
most advanced stages.
I remember
one elderly man
with a leg
which had obviously
been gangrenous
for some time:
it was black and shriveled,
but the skin rippled
with life:
maggots.
I applied benzene,
which killed them
on contact.

PREPARATION S

A 32-year-old man
came to the E.R.
complaining of
"a screwdriver
up my rear end."
"How did it
get there?"
I asked.
"I was using it
to itch my hemorrhoids,"
he replied,
"and it slipped
out of
my grasp."

ASSUMPTIONS II

I am sitting in my wheelchair
at a busy downtown intersection,
waiting for the light to change—
I'm heading west.
A helpful pedestrian
comes up behind me
and quietly pushes me across—
heading south.

ASSUMPTIONS III

I am sitting in my wheelchair
at a busy downtown intersection,
waiting for the light to change.
I am going from my office
to the hospital
where I practice internal medicine.
A kind stranger,
while I wait,
presses a dollar
in my hand.

MORE ASSUMPTIONS

When I was a resident physician,
a woman
got on the elevator
with me, and
seeing my stethoscope,
cooed,
"Isn't that cute,
a toy stethoscope."
"Madam," I replied,
drawing myself
up to my full (seated)
height of 4'3",
"this is a *real* stethoscope,
and *I*
am a real doctor."
As luck would have it,
she and I
rode the elevator together
several more times
after this.
She always greeted me
deferentially:
"Good morning, *doctor*."

PRIORITIES

A grateful patient,
on discharge
from the hospital,
distributed presents:
To the med student
(with few patients,
ample time for each):
a watch.
To the resident
(busier, less time):
a shirt.
To me, attending physician
(least time of all):
breath mints.
For the patient
it was
time spent,
attention given
(not experience)
for which
he was most
grateful.

DELIVERANCE

When I was a young attending physician
at the hospital
where I had trained,
I got on the elevator
one morning
with a woman,
who greeted me warmly,
and her son.
"Don't you remember James?"
she asked,
indicating the boy.
"You delivered
him 8 years ago."

GOING HOME

Very ill patients
used to tell me
"I want to go home."
In no way were they
ready:
they knew this
and so did I,
making the request
puzzling.
Until I realized
what they really meant
was
"I want things to be
like they were
before I got sick,"
home being
the symbol
of that
other time.

HEALTHCARE

A friend
with numerous symptoms
and a doctor
for each
had a hard time
getting
an accurate
diagnosis.
In frustration,
he went to
his veterinarian,
described his symptoms,
gave a
urine specimen,
and was
promptly diagnosed
as having
diabetes.

LOSS

The nursing-home patient
had lost
a spouse,
her health,
her home,
her possessions,
her cat,
her future,
her belief in
life's fairness.
When her family
replaced her
worn housecoat,
the new one
was
soon stolen.

GREED?

The nursing-home patient
had lost
a spouse,
her health,
her home,
her possessions,
her cat,
her future,
her belief in
life's fairness.
When she
requested
a second pillow
she was told,
"You want
too much."

ROLE CONFUSION

As I was
concluding the admission physical
with a rectal exam,
the somewhat confused
older patient
rolled over,
looked at me,
looked at my wheelchair,
and asked,
"And what room
are you in,
dear?"

DYING

Patients say
they're afraid
of dying
but most aren't
afraid of being dead,
they're afraid
of the dying *process*:
dying short of breath . . . .
dying in pain . . . .
dying alone . . . .

MIND-BODY CONNECTIONS II

When patients have
psychosomatic complaints
and the doctor
brushes them off,
they feel
anxious,
abandoned,
misunderstood—
generating
even more
psychosomatic complaints.

MAGICAL THINKING

When I was an internist
many patients faithfully
kept their appointments
although doing nothing else
I recommended.
I didn't then understand
about "external locus of control":
they thought
just showing up
would magically
fix them.

BODY IMAGE

Often
when I am
in my car
or seated
on a couch,
wheelchair out of sight,
friends do not
recognize
me.
My wheelchair
has become
a part of *me*,
the body image
by which
I'm known.

PRESENCE

When I was in training
to be a psychiatrist
my supervisor told me
I practiced psychiatry
like an internist:
"always looking for
something to fix."
"Don't just do something,
stand there,"
was his advice.

A PUZZLE

"If you're crippled
and can't heal yourself,"
my paranoid schizophrenic
patient
wanted to know,
"how are you going
to help me?"

PERSONALITY

Our personalities
are a
complicated mix
of what we
started with,
and how that
was shaped
by loves experienced
and love lost
and by hurt
and failure
and joy
and dreams fulfilled,
and by defenses erected
and beliefs
and values,
and by the fear
and vulnerability
that come
with age—
A complex recipe
with even more
complex results.

SCREENS

The church I attend
installed a large screen
in the sanctuary
last month:
the sermons have now
gone from
audio
to video.
Screens are everywhere
these days—
in our homes,
on our phones,
in our cars:
transitional objects,
soothing and calming us,
ensuring we
need never
feel alone.

ASSUMPTIONS IV

My colleague,
a black psychiatrist,
went to the E.R.
for complications
of her pregnancy.
"May I please see your
Medicaid card,"
the clerk there
requested.

DOWNHILL SPIRAL

My patient,
growing up in a household
of neglect and abuse,
wounded,
developed a needy demandingness
that drove others away,
the reward for woundedness
being more woundedness.

THE DEVIL'S DEED

The schizophrenic patient
told the staff
repeatedly,
"The Devil
is gnawing
on my womb."
"A somatic delusion,"
the staff
repeatedly
told one another.
To mollify the patient,
a pelvic exam
was done.
The patient had
carcinoma
of the uterus.
She just interpreted
and expressed
her symptoms
in a psychotic
way.

CONSCIENTIOUSNESS II

A med student was asked
by the E.R. staff
to evaluate a patient
for depression.
The patient, a young woman,
was complaining of
fatigue, insomnia and weight loss.
"Why can't you sleep?"
the student asked.
"Because I get up
eight times a night
to pee," she was told.
The patient wasn't depressed;
she had diabetes.
The student wasn't
unusually wise or experienced:
she just took
a thorough
history.

STIGMA

She seems unusually
cheerful
for someone just diagnosed
with M.S.
When I question her—
"I'm not crazy after all,"
she enthuses,
"I have a real disease.
They had been treating me
for three years for
psychosomatic illness."

ALLERGIES

My neighbor,
an allergist,
frequently told the parents
of his young patients
"He's got allergies;
you'll have to
get rid
of the dog."
When my neighbor
took his own dog
to the vet,
the vet
was pleased
to tell him,
"Your dog has
allergies,
you'll have to
get rid of
the children."

YOU CAN'T GO HOME AGAIN

When I returned to Texas
after 40 years away
I felt I had
finally
come home.
Texans listened
to my accent
and asked,
"You're not
from around here,
are you?"

THE KINDNESS OF STRANGERS

I am new in town
just over a year
with few
close friends yet.
I return from the O.R.
to my hospital room
and there discover
eighteen floral arrangements
and ten cards.

LEFT BRAIN

"Is that something significant,
or something trivial?"
her engineer father asked
after learning
of her double mastectomy
for breast
cancer.

TRANSCENDENCE

The colors of the flowers,
stained glass.
The tree limbs,
gothic arches.
The squirrels,
gargoyles,
gracing the cathedral
of my garden,
lifting my heart
to You.

RAIN

The storm has passed,
leaving the bushes
covered with
5-carat raindrops,
perfect in
color and
clarity.

DE NILE

My patient had
all the complications
of severe alcoholism
but continued to deny
that drinking
was a problem.
"How much do you drink
a day?" I asked.
"A case and a half
of Pearl Lite," he replied,
"the closest thing to water
you can buy."

ETHICAL DILEMMA

A woman
undergoing fertility treatment
was accidentally
implanted with
another couple's embryo.
"Sue the doctor,"
they said.
"Abort,"
they said.
She chose
to continue the pregnancy,
giving the baby
to the
other
couple.

THE DEVIL'S BARGAIN

She was a woman
of talent,
beauty,
possibility.
"Marry me,"
he said,
"and all you want
can be
yours.
You'll never
have to work
again."
The promise proved
less a paradise
and more
an airless
tomb.

SERIAL FORGIVENESS

A mother
whose daughter
was murdered,
interviewed on TV,
was asked
about anger.
"You've heard the expression
'forgive and forget'?"
she asked.
"I forgive,
and when I forget
I've forgiven,
I forgive
again."

A CONFLICT

Being ill
has an etiquette
all its own.
If you complain,
you fear you'll
be seen as
a whiner . . . .
. . . upset your family . . . .
. . . drive away your caregivers.
But if you say "I'm fine,"
you cut off
all authentic
dialogue,
leaving yourself
to carry
all the pain
alone.

HIGH STANDARDS

When my patient was in college
her father frequently criticized
her bad grades:
"Stop going to plays and
ballets," he directed,
"and *study*."
One of his most scathing
letters arrived
the fall of her senior year,
a week before
her election to
Phi
Beta
Kappa.

SUSPICION

Paranoid patients
sometimes think I'm
feigning disability
so they'll
feel sorry for me
and let their
defenses down.
They tell me so
very bluntly:
"I know
what you're up to.
You're not
fooling me."

PET THERAPY

It's said that animals give us
unconditional love,
and they do.
But we can also
love *them*
with our whole hearts,
holding nothing back,
never needing to fear
being betrayed.

DIFFICULT PATIENTS

Doctors label patients
"difficult"
when they break
an unwritten contract.
The contract says
the patient will be
compliant and respectful,
the doctor will be
skillful and caring,
the patient will
get better
and be grateful,
and everyone
will feel good.
"Difficult" patients
break the contract,
sometimes only by
not getting
better.

A MATTER OF PERSPECTIVE

The elderly man
had recently
lost his wife
and was
quite depressed.
"How long
were you
married?"
my colleague asked.
"Sixty-two years," he said.
"A long time," she replied.
"Not long enough,"
his rueful
response.

FAMILY

Since I have no children,
my job became my children:
the patients I treat,
the doctors I train.
When my husband died,
my job became my spouse,
my first love.
When my parents died,
my job became my parents.
What will happen
when I have to
retire?

BURNOUT

A sure sign of burnout
is when we start
to regard
the people we serve
as adversaries:
police officers, civilians;
teachers, students;
pastors, parishioners;
doctors, patients.
We've encountered
enough
difficult people
that we assume
everyone
will prove difficult,
usually
a self-fulfilling
prophecy.

RESIDENT PHYSICIANS

The residents I trained
when I worked
full time
were my professional
children—
I supervised, directed,
criticized if need be.
The residents I teach
in retirement
are professional
grandchildren.
Let the younger staff
do the criticizing
and directing now—
I'm in it
purely for
the pleasure.

UNANSWERABLE

My mother
lay in a nursing home bed
eighteen months
confused
incontinent
frightened
before she died.
Why?

A DEPRESSION SURVIVOR

When my father was dying,
he announced he was
going to find a wife.
"To cook
and iron my shirts,
and sew on buttons,"
he added.
"It sounds like you
need a housekeeper,
Dad,"
I said.
"Housekeepers cost
$25 an hour,"
his reply.

FUNERAL

He'd made it
to 95,
outlasting friends
and family.
Those he'd
influenced —
and there were
many —
were mostly
gone now,
too.

There was no service.

A funeral,
or its lack,
inaccurately
reflects
the value
of a life.

YOUTH VS. AGE

As a twenty-something
paraplegic
I was often
praised for my
courage and bravery,
something that
at sixty-something
no longer happens.
Now I'm just one more
"senior" with
"mobility issues":
disability earns
extra credit
in the young
by being age-inappropriate.

AGING

When I turned 60,
I suddenly
became interested
in the high school classmates
I had not seen
in over 40 years . . . .
. . . puzzling.
Philip Roth
helped me understand:
I wanted to see
how all those stories
had turned out,
and re-live in memory
a time when
life seemed infinite
and possibilities
without limit.

THREE WORDS

A 64-year-old school bus driver
was killed
in a collision
with an 18-wheeler.
A friend,
interviewed for the paper,
said of
the man's life,
"You could summarize it as
'family, church, and fishing'."

Sixty-four years,
three words.

BETRAYAL

Once our bodies
have betrayed
us,
it's hard to feel
really safe
again.
There's a vulnerability
as we scan
the road ahead,
fearing what
lies around
that
next corner.
Sometimes the fear
is worse
than
the illness.

DEATH

A friend encountered Death today,
who thus confronted me.
I hadn't thought his presence yet
so near to me to see.

And yet my sorrow's not for her,
she's now at peace, you see,
but rather for my own close glimpse
of my mortality.

INTIMATIONS . . . .

The doctor calls them PVC's*
but what they are to me:
a gentle tapping on my chest
of my mortality.

*a type of irregular heartbeat

ARMOR

Away at school
for the first time,
she tried
when the homesickness
was worst
to recall situations
where her mother
had treated her
unfairly.
The anger
and righteous indignation
dispelled the pain,
and felt more powerful
than
longing.
Unlearning love
became her style
of
self-protection.

ARMOR II

When tragedy follows
happiness,
we sometimes conclude
the happiness caused
the tragedy—
some perverse
balancing of the scales—
and vow never again
to fully experience joy
lest we again
be broadsided by
sorrow.

PRECEDENT

When I told the patient
I would have to
put a catheter
in his bladder,
his terror
and resistance
seemed extreme.
Yet he was calm
during the procedure.
"It's much easier
when you put
that greasy stuff
on the catheter first,"
he afterwards
gratefully
commented.

TIMING

A friend died
last week
in the prime of life:
active, vibrant,
engaged.
Others die
after protracted
incapacity
and suffering.
A colleague
once told me
people die either
too soon
or too late.
No one ever dies
right
on time.

PAIN

Why don't doctors
believe in pain?
If the patient says
his pain is
a nine,
the doctor thinks cynically
to himself,
"Yeah, probably more like
a four."
And it's often not for lack
of education,
or for fear of being
manipulated
for narcotics,
or even because the doctor
has never had pain
himself.
Although we believe
in other things
which can't be measured,
when it comes to pain
doctors seem to be
at heart
agnostic.

TOO LITTLE INFORMATION

A newspaper story
in its entirety
reported that
a one-hundred-year-old
nursing home resident
was found dead.
An autopsy was done.
(Why?)
It showed
she had been strangled.
End of story.
How?
By whom?
Why?

TRANSFERENCE

When we're sick
we become like
needy children.
When the appointment clerk
is brusque,
or the secretary
puts us on hold,
we're not just
frustrated
by "the system,"
but feel the special care
merited by our illness
has been denied,
and respond like children
of an uncaring
parent.

MATURITY?

When I consider
the petty slights,
resentments
and conflicts
which sometimes seem
to dominate my life,
I see myself
at sixty-five
as only a slightly greyer,
frailer
seven-
year-old.

TEXAS

Shortly after I moved
from Philadelphia
to Texas,
a patient was admitted
to our hospital
after his stallion
tore off his left arm.
Not long afterwards,
a clinic patient
told me the names
and personalities
of all her cows,
while another
gave her occupation
as "turkey sexer."
This wasn't
Philadelphia
any longer!

COLLECTORS

Some people collect hurts
the way others
collect stamps,
pasting the hurts
in their album
and taking them out
often
to be studied
and admired.
Their righteous indignation
feels like virtue,
and is almost as good as
happiness.

HUMANNESS

The poignancy of a diagnosis
is often lessened
by its commonness.
Strokes are like that,
although more so
than diagnoses of cancer
or heart disease.
Perhaps because strokes
affect the mind,
the personality,
the very *self*,
stroke patients
are sometimes seen
as less human than before,
and responded to
accordingly.

DISSATISFACTION

When a patient returns
repeatedly
with the same unresolved complaint,
the doctor grows frustrated
and subliminally
sends a message
to the patient
saying,
"Go away,"
instead of saying
to himself,
"What might I
be missing
here?"

GEOGRAPHIC CURE

When our lives
are going badly,
we sometimes decide
to change them
by moving far away.
Unfortunately,
when we do,
we bring ourselves
with us.

BEING KNOWN

Medical students are often afraid
to ask personal questions
for fear of offending
the patient.
I tell them
we can ask anything—
anything at all—
if we ask
with care, concern,
compassion.
Patients, like the rest of us,
yearn to be
known.

ERRORS

A serial killer in England,
a physician,
was convicted of murdering
fifteen patients.
Yet many of his patients
continued to
support and encourage him.
I too have seen cases
where patients forgive
the most egregious errors
committed by their doctors,
as long as they perceive the doctors
as
kind and caring.

ME

When I was hospitalized
for my spinal cord injury
and struggling with
the physical losses,
my doctor said one morning,
"Yes, but you're still you."
He was right;
there is an inner self
which totally transcends
the body self.
I still see as saddest
those illnesses
in which the patient
can no longer say,
"Yes, but I've still got
me."

UNCERTAINTY

One of the tolls illness takes
is having to live with uncertainty,
and with the realization we're "no longer"
in control.
What will the biopsy show?
When will I have my next seizure?
What if the medicine doesn't work?
Some patients even prefer
bad news
to the limbo of
not knowing.

BURDEN

Patients sometimes talk
about not wanting to
be a burden.
Besides the altruism,
what some also mean is
"I don't want to become
such a burden
I end up being
left."

ILLUSION

"Growing Old is a Choice,"
the AARP bulletin trumpets
in bold letters.
Apparently the cost
of maintaining this illusion
must be borne
by the hapless aged,
blamed for
choosing
poorly.

LIVING TOO LONG

Nursing home patients sometimes say,
"I've lived too long."
Some mean it
just that way,
while for others the statement,
made with humor,
is a convoluted form of bragging,
while still acknowledging
societal prejudice
against excessive age.
Some use the statement
as a veiled question,
the hoped-for answer being
"No, of course you haven't."

BOTTOM LINE

In 1980, medical news
began being reported
on the business page of the paper—
a sea-change for healthcare delivery.
Entrepreneurial medicine
is now everywhere:
the bottom line is
the bottom line.
At what cost to
the profession?
At what cost to
the patient?
At what cost to
our humanity?

RESILIENCE

The current trend,
when crisis strikes,
is to drive in
a busload of therapists
to help people "cope,"
implying they couldn't do so
on their own.
My experience is very different:
most people cope
perfectly well
using traditional resources
of family, friends and faith,
and in the process experience
one of the unadvertised gifts
of crisis:
discovering their own
unsuspected strength.

SELF-IMAGE

Illness may radically change
self-image—
attractiveness, lovableness, sexuality.
Young spinal-injured patients
sometimes say they're no longer men,
no longer women,
but a "third sex,"
neuters.
It's another facet of
their loss.

COPING

"Coping" proceeds at its own pace.
One young man,
after a paralyzing injury,
sat in front of the T.V.
for nine years
before he announced one day
to his family,
"This sucks,
I'm going to law school,"
and did.

HIDING

When life is painful,
we hide our pain,
wanting to
still be seen
as strong, brave.
Sometimes we've learned
others don't want
to hear our pain.
And pain shames us,
making us feel like
non-contenders,
losers.
Since hurt and loss
touch us all,
why do we turn and hide,
as though we were the
only ones?

HUBRIS II

Part of training to be a physician
involves learning to
project confidence and authority
in the face of
incomplete knowledge
and uncertainty.
If the doctor is not careful,
he begins to buy into
his own omniscience,
developing a
destructive
hubris.

SYMPTOMS

Serious illness often hits hard
right from the outset—
a sudden severe pain,
or the discovery of a tell-tale lump.
Other times it tiptoes up
almost soundlessly—
like with my friend
whose only hint of trouble
was watering of one eye,
the first sign a lymphoma
had invaded her tear duct.
Knowing which"innocent" symptom
to take seriously
and which not
can sometimes be a challenge
for both doctor and patient.

FOCUS

Sometimes when I'm stressed
and being pulled in different directions,
if I ask—not—
"What do *I* want?'"—
But—
(something usually very different)—
"What is best for this situation?"
it helps me focus and
prioritize.

WHERE YOU SIT DETERMINES
WHERE YOU STAND

A clinician I was seeing
had an impeccable
bedside manner.
He listened, didn't interrupt,
encouraged questions.
When I complimented him,
he replied,
"I wasn't always like this,"
adding that his approach
to patients changed
when he himself became a patient
diagnosed with a
serious illness
and discovered what patients
really need.

HUBRIS III

A gynecologist,
explaining to my friend the
protective functions of
the normal vaginal flora,
said,
"You see, Lisa, it's like there
are thousands of little policemen
patrolling inside your vagina… ."
What he seems not
to have noticed
is my friend's Ph.D.
in Science.

MOTIVES

Sometimes when we do a good deed,
it is less out of genuine affection
for the recipient,
and more for the feeling of being good
by doing good.
The recipient, hoping for friendship,
responds by reaching out to us
and is puzzled by our
reticence.

MEDICAL LIBRARY

Asked for an oxymoron,
I usually give the timeworn
"military intelligence,"
although I recently heard
a better example:
"paperless library."

BIRTHDAYS

After over three decades
in Philadelphia,
on my fiftieth birthday I moved
to Texas.
Birthdays ending in zero are
like that—
the start of a new decade
gets our attention,
inviting reappraisal and sometimes
dramatic change.

ANIMAL SHELTER

Volunteers in animal shelters
have sometimes grown disenchanted
with people.
Animals are safer.
They need us.
We're in control.

PROJECTIVE IDENTIFICATION

Volunteers in animal shelters
identify with frightened,
injured animals.
Helping hurt animals,
they vicariously
heal their own hurts.

Doctors sometimes do the same.

CAREER CHOICE

We sometimes pick a profession
which provides
something missing in our lives
up to then—
power, or respect,
or love.

INCUBATION

It's been said a writer is
someone who can't help writing.
At an earlier stage, though,
a writer may be someone
who yearns to write
but can't,
having not yet found
her voice.

DIFFICULT PATIENTS II

Things we take personally usually
aren't personal.
The patient is either scared or angry,
or lacks social skills,
or typically treats everyone
this way.
Despite our sensitivity,
it's often not
about us.

DOUBLE BIND

One of the challenges of being hospitalized
is having your most basic needs
delegated to others
who fail to provide them.
Like getting a bed pan
in a timely fashion,
or a pain pill
when you're hurting.
The patient, who did not ask to
relinquish his autonomy,
is now chastised for
his dependence:
"I'm taking care of someone else right
now. You're not my
only patient."

DREAMS

Doctors long retired
still have dreams about medicine:
surgeons operate nightly,
internists ponder diagnostic
possibilities,
the triumphs and terrors of
internships long past
are relived
during sleep.
Do salesmen when retired
still dream of
selling cars?

EXCLUSIVITY

We enjoy being connected with
groups and places which are
"exclusive,"
which is to say,
which exclude others.
Is our sense of self
so tenuous
it hinges on
the number of people
to whom we feel
superior?

COUNTERTRANSFERENCE

Narcissistic patients talk *at* you,
not *with* you.
I was always tempted to
put a life-size cardboard cutout
of myself
in the doctor's chair
and take a fifty-minute coffee break,
suspecting the patient may not
even notice.

APPEARANCES

People are often judged by
what they have—
or even *seem* to have—
appearance being more important
than reality.
Outward bling, inward
bankruptcy.

APPEARANCES II

At Starbucks, a friend
noticed a man
who looked
down on his luck.
About to buy him coffee,
my friend hesitated
as the man
handed the clerk two dollars
and requested a copy of the
New York Times.

TIME

Who is the grizzled stranger
who greets me each morning
from my bathroom mirror?
And what's become
of the smiling 35 year old
of only a few days past?

Time is a constant presence now,
its awareness
dimming the sunlight
which falls on the
concluding chapters
of my story.

BEYOND ALL WORDS

A much beloved
Salvation Army worker is
murdered on Christmas eve
for the money in
his kettle,
while his young
children watch.
On Christmas day,
a micro-chipped dog,
someone's pet,
is cut open
and left dying
at a veterinarian's door.
How does a season of
peace and love
spawn such
evil?

INSOMNIA

Hospitalized patients
sometimes can't sleep—
they don't want to—
letting down their guard
is risky—
they need to stay awake
and Watch.

SILVER LINING

When people are ill or
in crisis,
they relate to others
with an authenticity present
at no other time.
Facades crumble,
trivia falls away,
hearts connect—
a hidden gift of
tragedy.

WRESTLER

A doctor friend was examining
an ex-wrestler.
Thorough as ever,
he was concluding
with a rectal exam when
the patient asked him,
"Doc, can you teach me
that hold?"

CONNECTION

Twitter, texting, games at parties
seem to be ways of
feeling connected
without the risks
(or work)
of real intimacy.
Or is it that
we're all surface—
no depth—
no "there" there
to be intimate
with?

BEAUTY

We spend lavishly
on beautifying our
hair, eyes, teeth, skin, lips,
breasts, muscles, nails,
feet—
imagine if we spent
as lavishly
beautifying our
souls!

BEAUTY II

We spend lavishly
on beautifying our
hair, eyes, teeth, skin, lips
breasts, muscles, nails,
feet—
if we believed we had a soul
to beautify,
would we lavish as much
on it?

PAIN II

Patients in chronic pain
sometimes let pain
structure their lives and
define who they are.
Cure can be scary,
threatening both
identity
and lifestyle.

LONGING

My patient,
embracing the saying
"Happiness is never wanting what
you can't have,"
had so deeply repressed
her true desire
that only in receiving it
did she powerfully realize
the depth and duration
of her longing.

BIOGRAPHY

My librarian friend says
a home library is often
a brief biography of
its owner:
Little Women, Lady Chatterley's Lover,
The World's Great Religions, Dr. Spock,
Making the Most of Your Money, You and
Your Second Marriage, Passages,
Aging Well, Ivan Ilych,
Death and Dying.

DENIAL

Denial is a normal part of
serious illness,
yet people want to
strip it away
too soon:
"Don't you realize you
have CANCER?!"
Denial is like a scab
covering a wound,
protecting the delicate tissue
underneath as
it heals.
When the healing is complete,
the scab drops away
of its own accord.

POWER

My doctor friend,
a former hospital C.E.O.,
was used to being greeted
frequently and
deferentially
as he walked the hospital corridors.
Now retired,
he is rarely greeted at all:
the constantly changing staff
no longer knows him—
the evanescence of power.

YOKED

Patients with suicidal thoughts
feel less troubled
after sharing these thoughts
with their doctor.
It's as though someone has
slipped under the yoke
with them,
sharing the burden.
Feeling yoked to
someone else,
less alone,
they're less likely to
give up
on life.

YOKED II

Patients with chronic illness
feel less troubled
after sharing their symptoms with
the doctor.
They're not requesting
cure, or even relief,
just the reassurance
that they need not
shoulder their burden
all alone.

ASSUMPTIONS V

A newcomer at church,
focusing on my wheelchair,
asked sympathetically
what I did to
pass the time.
"Besides practicing medicine,
you mean?"
I inquired.

DEBTS

My patient was unwilling to
accept presents;
but if she had to,
she immediately bought a gift
for the other person,
cancelling the debt.
She wanted to be independent,
self-sufficient, needing and
beholden to
no one.

GIFTS

My patient,
unable to accept gifts
but sometimes forced to,
unconsciously solved her
dilemma
by never liking the gift.
"I'll take it back on
Monday,"
she would say.

WITHDRAWAL

My patient had an
unwritten contract
with life:
"I will never make
any requests of you,
but in return
I expect no requests to be made of me."
In times long past,
her requests had too often
been forgotten or
denied.

HELP

Disabled patients
sometimes feel that
accepting help
is proof of inadequacy.
When, out of kindness,
help is forced
on them,
it can feel intrusive,
further evidence of
their perceived
inability.

BUSYNESS

A retired friend describes
her busyness:
aerobics class, genealogy club,
lunch with friends,
volunteer job, synagogue committees,
Neighborhood Watch—
and yet there's a driven-ness to it,
a compulsivity,
an absence of real pleasure.
What is she
looking for?
What is she
running from?

RE-EVALUATION

Life rarely gives us
respites,
times without activities or obligations.
Illness is one such time,
and can be an occasion
for solitude, introspection,
reassessment.
Major life changes
are sometimes first considered
and initiated
when ill.

POSSIBILITY

In youth,
possibilities are endless;
choosing among them,
we begin to live.
But each choice narrows further choice,
and,
savoring possibility,
we rebel:
"I'll start again,"
we say:
new marriage, new
career,
new city,
another chance at
youth.

DOCTORS

The competitive perfectionism
which gets us into
medical school
and insures our success
is also our
surest cause of
burnout.

RELATIONSHIP

What heals in medicine,
besides knowledge and skills,
is relationship:
to be known, to be
understood,
to be
cared about.
Doctors are not
interchangeable.

VEHICLE

Our bodies are
our vehicles
for the journey of life.
If the vehicle
has an uncomfortable ride,
or breaks down unpredictably
requiring expensive repairs,
or causes people to stare:
"Ooh, look at *that* clunker!"
the journey is not quite
as pleasant.

QUERY

Is it better to happily
lead a superficial,
unexamined life,
or to ponder deeply
issues of
God, pain, meaning,
identity, death—
and suffer?

Is the suffering"depression"?
Is the cure a pill?

ETHICAL DILEMMA II

A fifty-four-year-old man,
retarded, blind, deaf,
institutionalized
since birth,
developed cancer.
"Chemotherapy,"
the oncologist recommended,
"It could give him
another
two years."

BIAS

The health complaints of patients with
mental illness
are often greatly discounted.
Even dramatic symptoms
such as
vomiting blood or crushing
chest pain are
attributed to"imagination"
or "psychosis."
Patients on antidepressants for
non-psychiatric symptoms
such as pain
can experience the same bias.
The bias is a dualistic
one,
favoring "matter" over
"mind,"
"real illness" over the
mental kind.

BATTLE

The struggle with illness
is a battle between
two adversaries,
the doctor and death.
Each victory enhances
the doctor's sense of
omnipotence.
Sometimes the doctor's
primary motivator
is the battle,
care or cure of the *patient*
representing
mere incidentals.

BATTLE II

Issues of appropriateness
of care
are easily overlooked
if the doctor's primary motivation
is the battle with death,
and the patient represents
only
the venue.

DRAMA

Names on a prayer chain,
hushed, breathless reports of
medical encounters,
flaunting of bandages,
scars,
hair loss:
for some patients, illness
is their main source
of importance and
drama.

CURE-ALL

In retirement, patients
lack a sense of power, authority,
agency.
Our culture provides the cure-all,
available for a variety
of psychic woes:
the power to choose, order, buy,
consume.

HEALED

On dialysis, awaiting a
kidney,
my patient was calm, accepting,
very much alive.
When I remarked
on this,
he said of his chronic illness,
"I may not be cured,
but I feel I've been healed."

ETHICS

In addition to considerations of
"beneficence,"
"non-maleficence,"
"what the patient would want,"
doctors sometimes wish
to let their irreversibly
damaged patients
"go"
because caring for them
is intrinsically
not satisfying.

WHITE COATS

Starched white coats
rarely stay that way long
in a busy hospital practice.
I always thought
a tie-dye pattern
of brown, yellow and red
would be more appropriate.

BEING VS. DOING

My neighbor,
knowing I am retired,
tells me that I'm
"not a doctor *anymore*."
She believes a doctor
is something you do,
not something you
are.

VEINS

Hospital staff
who start IV's
often blame the patient
if they miss the vein:
"You have bad veins,"
"Your veins roll,"
"Your veins are too deep."
I've never heard
anyone say
"Sorry—I'm not very
good at this."

DEBRIS

Leaves constantly blow under
my garage door.
As often as I sweep,
the garage never stays
swept and clean
for long.

Like my inner life.

FELINE EXISTENTIALISM

When my cats go to the vet,
a frightening car ride
is rewarded with shots
and other unpleasant procedures.
If cats thought about meaning,
they would probably interpret
lovingly-provided healthcare
as unmerited suffering
dispensed by their
unfeeling god.

PARENTS

When our parents
lose their power
and we no longer need
to rebel,
we can finally begin
to love.

HEARTBEAT

The loud rhythmic
thumping music
of a passing car radio
reminds me of a
Doppler recording
of a human heartbeat.
Is the music
an unconscious memory
of a long-ago
in-utero
soundtrack?

HOSPITAL GOWN

A hospital gown
appropriately symbolizes
the role it represents:
it removes all external cues
of status,
along with modesty and
self-possession,
and (by its skimpiness)
precludes walking freely
in the hospital halls.
An apt representation
of the loss of power, status
and autonomy
experienced
on becoming
a patient.

TIMOR MORTIS

When my father was dying,
and knew it,
he never discussed death,
but remarked quizzically
on his new inability to sleep
at night
without leaving the light
in the bedroom closet
burning.

FOREPLAY

Pacemakers,
colostomies,
amputations—
death's foreplay
before the eventual consummation.

PRESENCE II

I wish doctors would
stop telling their patients
that they "have nothing
more to offer."
We always have
something more to offer,
if only our ongoing
presence.

SCARS II

A surgeon I knew
took particular care
suturing the incision once
the surgery was done.
"It's my signature
on the patient's belly,"
he told me,
"and will last
a lifetime."